SO YOU WANT TO BE A
KNIGHT?

Written by
HANNAH PANG

Illustrated by
TAKAYO AKIYAMA

Inspired by the book by
MICHAEL PRESTWICH

T&H

First published in the United States of America in 2021
by Thames & Hudson Inc., 500 Fifth Avenue, New York,
New York 10110

So You Want To Be A Knight?
©2021 Thames & Hudson Ltd, London

Based on the book by Michael Prestwich
Knight ©2010 Thames & Hudson Ltd, London

Illustrations © 2021 Takayo Akiyama

Abridged from the original by Hannah Pang
Designed by Belinda Webster

Library of Congress Control Number 2020931417

ISBN 978-0-500-65211-4

Printed and bound in China by Everbest Printing Investment Ltd

Be the first to know about our new releases,
exclusive content and author events by visiting
thamesandhudson.com
thamesandhudsonusa.com
thamesandhudson.com.au

ROBERT THE BRUCE
Great Scot and King!

JOANNA OF FLANDERS, DUCHESS OF BRITTANY
Female warrior

These knights in armor are all really intimidating. That guy Geoffroi, the author—he sounds like a good guy.

OMG, LEGEND! She fought at the Siege of Hennebont, burning down the enemy camp.

7

WHERE TO START?

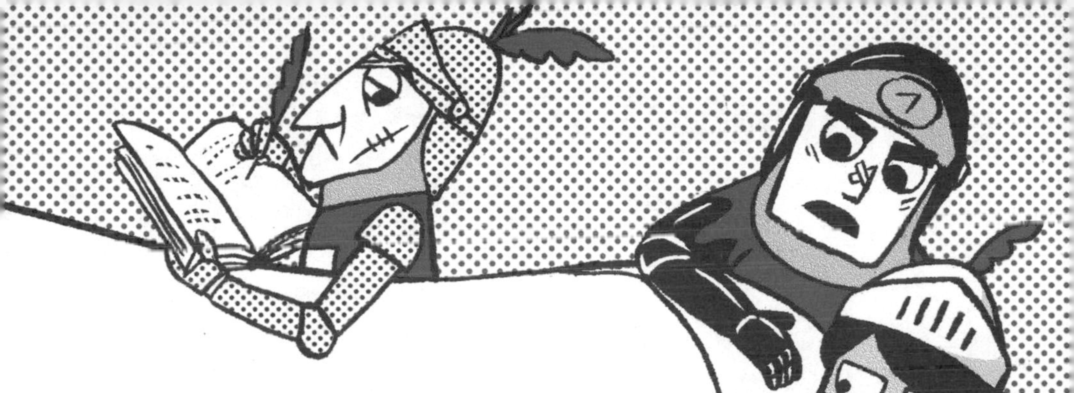

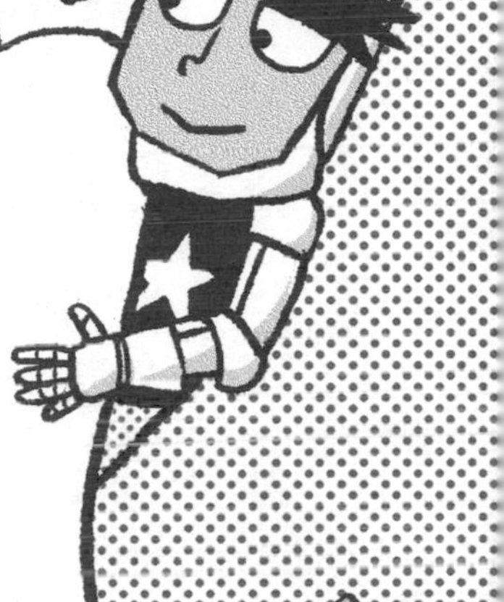

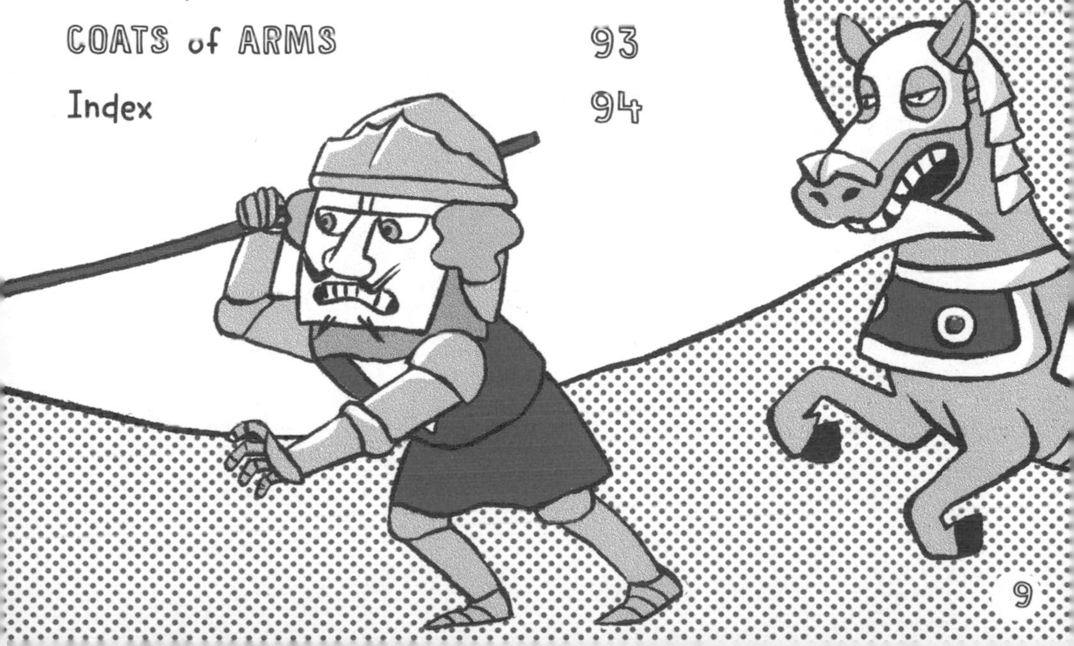

MEDIEVAL MUSINGS

Knights need to be so physically fit,

Now, that's not even the half of it!

Involve yourself in the "wine and dine"–then

Gallop away on your horse in good time!

Honor your friends, and kill all your foes,

Train 'til you can't feel your fingers or toes!

So, do you still want to be a knight?
You must go into battle and you cannot be scared.
Or, at least read this book–and go well prepared!

I'm JOHN.
I don't have a special title or a fancy name—but I'm so good at fighting, I worked my way up the ranks to become the most respected knight in England. Take this simple test to see if you too can gain fame and fortune as a knight.

KNIGHT CHECKLIST

Tick all boxes that apply ☑

1. I HAVE GOOD BREEDING ☑

While not essential (just look at John!), having noble blood really helps. Knighthood tends to run in families. If your father was a knight, then you shouldn't have too much trouble becoming one too!

You're just like your father!

You will also need to understand how to behave in the right way and how to fit into the upper-class world. This means remembering your "p's and q's"!

2. I HAVE BAGS OF MONEY

Taking part in crusades is expensive. As a leader, you will
need enough money to hire 30,000 men to make an army
(who all need to be fed and watered). Then there's
all the equipment to pay for—plus any ransoms. And if you
spend too much, you'll have to abandon the whole idea!

> Oh no. I'm down
> to my last bag of coins
> and I only have
> an army of 5.

3. I CAN READ A COAT OF ARMS

Coats of arms carry important messages about the
wearer—a bit like sports team logos. You need to
study them carefully. Learn friend from foe and it
could save your life one day! When you design your
own coat of arms, make sure that it is original.

> Watch out!
> I'm dangerously cute!

> ....

4. I'VE GOT THE MOVES

Your skills aren't just for the battlefield—you'll need to impress on the dance floor too!

✔

5. I HAVE A BUSINESS HEAD

Ransoming prisoners, bribery, horse-trading, wage rates, contracts, tax, bla, bla, bla—bored yet? If the answer is YES, then you better axe your armor.

✔

RANSOM NOTE
FREE
YOUR PRISONERS
FOR THE
BARGAIN PRICE
OF 200,000
GOLD FLORINS.

Yours sincerely,
your enemy.

6. I DON'T MIND BLOOD

Needless to say, this is a must!

✔

7. I CAN RIDE A HORSE

Many battles are won on horseback, so you'll need to learn how to control your horse!

8. I AM FIT FOR WEAPONS

You will need to be physically fit for grueling campaigns—fighting with weapons that require great skill, such as the lance and sword. Practice makes perfect!

Knights in training! I'm **LADY BOURBON**. I may look like a damsel in distress, but in fact I am a medieval influencer. To achieve fame and fortune in your career as a knight, you'll need to join an order, which is a type of special members' club. Take my quiz to find out which order suits you best, and then leave the rest to me...

WHICH ORDER WILL YOU JOIN?

1. CHOOSE YOUR DREAM VACATION

A — A trip around Europe, paid for by the order

B — A Baltic cruise

C — Sunning it in Greece

D — Relaxing in the English countryside

2. HOW DO YOU FEEL ABOUT MONEY?

A — The more the better!

B — I don't mind being out of pocket.

C — Who needs money, when you have the gift of life?

D — I prefer solid gold!

3. WHICH BEST DESCRIBES YOU?

A

B

C

D

I'm a little silly!

I'm a bit of a rule-breaker!

I'm very disciplined.

I'm fair and treat everyone equally.

4. PICK YOUR FAVORITE OUTFIT!

A

B

C

D

A catsuit

A fine fur coat

A monk's robes

A feather crest

5. WHICH IS YOUR FAVORITE SUBJECT?

A

B

C

D

Business studies

Politics

Religion

English Literature

OUNT UP YOUR A, B, C AND D ANSWERS. CHECK THE RESULTS ON THE NEXT PAGE >>>

QUIZ RESULTS:

IF YOU CHOSE MOSTLY A'S
YOU'RE MOST LIKELY TO JOIN:
THE ORDER OF THE TEMPLE

Even though you like to be naughty, you can be sensible when you need to be. Welcome to the Order of the Temple! It's believed that this order was destroyed early in the 14th century, but rumor has it that it still exists... The Templars own a lot of land in Europe, and are very wealthy—although they have a strange obsession with cats...

MOSTLY B'S
THE TEUTONIC KNIGHTS

The Teutonic Knights are so well-organized that they even have their own government. If you like outdoor feasts, hunting and jousting, then this is the order for you—just don't expect to get rich quick. Originally the Teutonic Knights set out to fight in the Holy Land, but they changed course for Lithuania. There are less riches to win, but the lifestyle is fantastic.

MOSTLY C'S:
THE ORDER OF THE HOSPITAL

This order has taken over much of the property from the Templars and is now based in Rhodes, Greece. Members are part monk, part knight. So pack up your armor and robes and mosey on down to the Mediterranean if you fancy a life of discipline under the sun.

MOSTLY D'S:
ORDER OF THE ROUND TABLE

This small, exclusive order has since changed its name to a slightly odd one: the Order of the Garter. Originally created in 1348 by Edward III of England, this order was based on the legend of King Arthur (Edward even built a huge round house with a round table in Windsor Castle for the knights to meet at).

WELCOME TO KNIGHT SCHOOL

LESSON #1

WEAPONS BEFORE WEANING

As a knight you will need to learn many skills, including how to use weapons—and you'll need to start young. Begin by using sticks as toy swords. Or follow King Edward I's lead—he gave his sons a miniature siege engine to play with!

LESSON #2
READING AND WRITING

There's more to war than looking good on a horse! A true knight must be able to read and write. There are muster rolls to be kept, orders to be read out and agreements to be made. While there are clerks to do these things, you will still need to double-check their work.

Are you sure that's how you spell "cavalry"?

LESSON #3
LANCE PRACTICE

The lance is a difficult weapon. It takes great skill just to hold the point steady, let alone aim it correctly. Before trying this on horseback, ask your friends to pull you along in a small cart for practice.

CERTIFICATE
WELL DONE!
YOU'RE READY TO GO TO WAR!

NOW THAT YOU CAN WALK THE WALK, AND TALK THE TALK, THE FINAL STAGE OF TRAINING IS TO GET SOME CAMPAIGNING EXPERIENCE UNDER YOUR BELT. CHILDREN CAN BE TAKEN TO WAR AT QUITE A YOUNG AGE— JOHN OF GAUNT WAS ONLY 10 YEARS OLD WHEN HE WATCHED HIS FATHER AND BROTHER, THE BLACK PRINCE, FIGHTING IN BATTLE IN 1350!

I'll take that!

HORSING AROUND

While you'll probably fight more on foot than on horseback, it is impossible to imagine a knight without a horse. As the French legal expert Honoré Bouvet said: "A knight is bold, too, by reason of his horse in which he has complete trust." In other words, get to know your horse—the two of you should act as one!

Psst! Hey you— it's JO here again. I came from an aristocratic family, so riding is my thing!

(My family thinks I married a nobleman in Scotland, and that I died from a broken heart when my pony passed away—but that's another story...)

JOANNE'S HOT-TO-TROT RIDING TIPS
Here are my top tips for horsing around...

TIP #1
Greet your horse nicely, and the odd treat won't go amiss!

TIP #2

Mount your horse with confidence, otherwise the horse will feel your nerves!

TIP #3

Keep a straight back at all times, in order to keep your balance. This will also help keep the saddle on straight—there's nothing worse than a lopsided ride!

TIP #4

Don't be too hard with the bit and spurs. How would you like to be prodded in the ribs every time you slowed for a breather?

PHYSICAL FITNESS

A good knight needs to have physical strength and stamina—in part just to carry your own armor and weapons. Follow the daily routine of the French knight Boucicaut and you'll be well on your way to being fit enough for a knighthood.

5 A.M.

Go for a long-distance run. Try to make it a bit longer each day, until you have what it takes to run for your life!

(Remember, you can't stop for a breather on the battlefield.)

10 A.M.
(YOU'LL NEED TIME FOR THAT LONG RUN!)

Practice jumping into the saddle of your horse from the ground. It's harder than it sounds...

12 P.M.
Next, it's time to practice somersaults while wearing full armor (you can remove your helmet if you need to).

I wish I hadn't just eaten my lunch.

8 P.M.
Start lifting weights in order to build up the strength in your arms. Carrying a heavy sword around is tougher than you think!

9 P.M.
While wearing a steel breastplate, climb the reverse side of a ladder hand over hand, without using your feet.

10 P.M.
Lastly, remove your armor, and do the same thing with the ladder—but with just one hand this time!

This is my worst nightmare times 100.

And I thought the jungle gym was hard enough...

KNIGHTLY HEROES

True knights are in a league of their own. What qualities inspire you to become the best knight you can be? Compare these knights and choose who is your hero!

CHIVALRY 100
FITNESS 60
RIDING 80
BATTLE 95

GEOFFROI DE CHARNY

A French knight, most famous for his "Book of Chivalry." His career began in 1337, when the war between England and France started. Captured by the English and ransomed, not once— but twice! A strategic war planner, who's also willing to play dirty.

CHIVALRY 95
FITNESS 70
RIDING 80
BATTLE 100

JOHN HAWKWOOD

An English knight, whose career began in France. Found fame and fortune in Italy. A soldier of immense ability (and popular with the ladies), John understands the complexities of war—turning any defeat into a triumph!

BOUCICAUT

CHIVALRY 80
FITNESS 100
RIDING 80
BATTLE 95

Wow!
These guys are like
the super squad!

Also known as Jean II Le Maingre, this French knight was only 12 when he went on his first campaign in Normandy in 1378—and was knighted just four years later!!! An exceptional athlete, both on and off the battlefield.

THE BLACK PRINCE

CHIVALRY 75
FITNESS 80
RIDING 100
BATTLE 95

Edward of Woodstock (aka the Black Prince) is the eldest son of King Edward III of England. Knighted by his father, as the English were about to land in Normandy in 1346. Has a good business head and can negotiate well. Can manage 25 miles a day on a horse!

25 miles a day
on a horse—
OUCH!

HOW TO BEHAVE

As well as being a good fighter, a knight has to be able to behave in the "correct" way. As it happens, I have written a best-selling guidebook on the subject...

TIP #1
SING LIKE A SONGBIRD

It helps if you can sing. Just imagine dazzling a damsel, or charming a king with a voice as melodious as a nightingale.

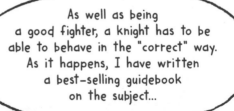

You're so bootiful! La la la! You're so strong! Do bee doo!

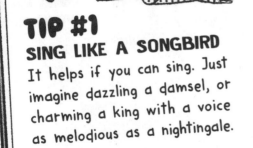

You're really good at this!

I know!

TIP #2
DANCE LIKE EVERYONE IS WATCHING

Take some dance classes. The courtly culture brings love songs and romances, plus dinners and dances. So you must be as comfortable on the dance floor as you are on the battlefield!

TIP #3
EAT WITH YOUR BEST MANNERS

When you're dining with others, follow the advice of Francesc Eiximenis: "If you have spat or blown your nose, never clean your hands on the table cloth."

At your service, Your Majesty.

TIP #4
BE CHIVALROUS

Chivalry is a set of values that all knights must uphold. To be chivalrous means to be generous, courteous, loyal and highly skilled. In other words, pay your army a good wage, be polite, don't betray your king and be really good at fighting.

REMEMBER: THESE SKILLS ARE COMPULSORY! THERE'S NO SUCH THING AS AN ORDINARY KNIGHT.

COATS OF ARMS

Now you are a knight, the real work can commence! First of all, you need a coat of arms. Not only does it help knights to identify each other—it also sends a message about a knight's family and connections in society.

> Oh, this is awkward...

1. BE ORIGINAL

If your family already has a coat of arms, change it slightly to show that you are blazing your own path. If your family doesn't have one, create your own design. Make sure it is original though—you don't want the same as someone else!

2. CHOOSE A BACKGROUND COLOR

Will it be red to show how passionate you are about the fight? Or white to signal innocence, purity and peace? Or blue to stand for your honesty and loyalty?

> I'm so PASSIONATE I would die for my horse!

> I'm for PEACE, especially if it means going home in one piece!

> If I'm honest, TRUTH is more my thing.

3. CHOOSE AN ORDINARY

Ordinaries divide a coat of arms into parts and help your charges, or symbols, stand out from the background.

PALE
I have great military strength

BEND
I am distinguished

FESS
I am ready to fight

CROSS
I am a Christian

CHIEF
I am a wise leader

CHEVRON
I have built houses and fortresses for my people

4. CHOOSE A CHARGE

A charge is an image that says something about you. What charge will you choose?

I am brave

I am powerful

I have endurance and am "hanging on"

I am wise

I am speedy

5. HAPPY WITH THE RESULT?

When you are on the battlefield, your coat of arms is like an avatar or logo. Does your coat of arms represent you accurately?

Angus—am I reading your coat of arms correctly: you're a peaceful hanger-on who wants to go home...?

GET KNIGHTED!

START HERE

1. DO YOU HAVE ENOUGH MONEY?

2. WILL YOU ACCEPT THE CHIVALRIC CODE?

YES

YES

NO

NO

WHAT DOES THAT EVEN MEAN?

START SAVING, OR GET SPONSORED
Being a knight is expensive! First, you need to buy your armor and weapons, and then a high-quality warhorse. None of these are things you want to skimp on...

THE CHIVALRIC CODE
You should only carry weapons for a just cause. For example, fighting for the Church, for your lord, or for your ancestors. If you're just in it for glory, then hang up your helmet now.

GO BACK TO THE LAST QUESTION!

UMM... SPEAK TO THE CAREERS DEPARTMENT?

3. ARE YOU READY TO CONFESS AND REPENT YOUR SINS?

YES

4. DO YOU LIKE LONG, HOT BATHS?

WHAT SINS?

NO

The day before you are knighted, you will need to take a bath. This is not to make you physically clean, but to cleanse you of your sins. You will never be naughty again...

YES

CONSIDER BECOMING A MERCENARY

(Turn to page 76 to find out more...)

NO

5. DO YOU LIKE DRESSING UP?

As well as being able to walk, ride and fight in heavy armor, a knight needs to dress up in the right outfit for the right moment. Stockings, tunics and spurs are just a few of a knight's must-have wardrobe items.

YES

How can you not like dress-ups?!

TURN OVER THE PAGE: YOUR CEREMONY IS ABOUT TO BEGIN!
>>>

LET THE CEREMONY BEGIN...

GET DRESSED

This is a once-in-a-lifetime event so make sure you turn up suited and booted—fellow knights will help you get dressed. Wear a red tunic to show you are ready to shed blood and black stockings to remind yourself that you're mortal. Accessorize with a white belt to show that you're pure, and a red cloak to show that you're humble.

Eddie, we can't help you get dressed if you won't let us see you in your underwear...

GO TO CHURCH

Now that you're dressed to impress, you have to sit through a long church service called a vigil. You'll stay up all night, thinking about the future you have ahead of you. But if that's too hard, just try to stay awake.

GET TAPPED

If you're still awake, the knighting ceremony will take place the next day. First, knights will fix some spurs to your shoes and give you yet another belt—this one is a symbol of your knighthood and is used to hold your sword. Another knight will then take a sword, kiss you on the cheek and tap you on the shoulder with the sword. Knighthood is only ever awarded by those who are excellent knights themselves.

That sword sure looks sharp!

GO TO BED

As a thank-you for your service, your king will give you some cloth to make your mantle—the tunic that goes over your suit of armor—along with a mattress and a quilt for your bedding. At last, you can get some sleep!

CONGRATULATIONS,
YOU ARE NOW A KNIGHT!!
Let's see how long you can keep your head!

BUY A SUIT OF ARMOR

You can either buy a suit of armor from an armorer who will make it to fit you exactly, or see if you can pick up some pieces secondhand. Either way, make sure it is the right size!

BACINET
- MOVEABLE VISOR: See and hear in battle!
- NEW FEATURE: Cone-shaped nose to let you breathe!

$$$

MAIL
- Genuine metal mail
- Literally thousands of links
- No more stab wounds
- NO GUARANTEE against crushing blows

$$$

CLOTH PADDING
- ESSENTIAL padding for under your mail
- Fight without chafing!

HOW TO GET INTO YOUR SUIT

Putting your armor on isn't as easy as it seems. You will need help from an attendant who knows which of the different parts goes where.

STEP 1

Light a fire—you'll need to stand in your underwear for some time and you don't want to freeze!

STEP 2

Put on some woollen tights and a tough padded jacket called an aketon. This has laces that come in handy in step 4.

STEP 3

Put on the metal mail that covers your head, body and legs.

STEP 4

Next put on the plate armor, including the cuirass which covers your chest and back. Your helper will buckle the plates up and lace each piece of armor to your aketon so it doesn't move.

STEP 5

Blow your nose and rub your eyes—it's time to put on your bacinet!

STEP 6

Step into your sabatons (armored boots) and gauntlets (gloves).

STEP 7

Lastly, pick up your sword— you're ready for action!

GIDDY UP, GET A HORSE!

Buying a horse will be one of the most important purchases of your knightly career. There are several different types of horse to choose from:

$100

SOLD

DESTRIER, OR CHARGER

Grandest horse of all. Large and powerful— 16 hands or more in height. Enjoy the occasional ride through the countryside and polish it on weekends! Best kept reserved for battle.

COURSER

Put the fun back into riding! A lighter horse, ideal for both war and tournaments. Great around town and easy to park!

So how much horsepower does this one have?

PALFREY
A riding horse, with a distinctive smooth gait. Very economical!

$5

$30

HACKNEY
Great British breed. Looks good! Also useful as a riding horse.

Oh no! The courser is sold! We would have been perfect for each other.

I think this one is about my height...

FREE TO A GOOD HOME

ROUNCEY
Just an ordinary horse.

41

ARM YOURSELF

Every knight needs a selection of weapons to attack and defend with, whether in a jousting tournament or at war. But remember, when you go to war, everything has to fit on one horse...

SWORD

The sword is an essential weapon for a knight. The perfect sword weighs no more than a large bag of sugar.

POMMEL
Stops the sword from sliding out of your hand.

HILT
A fancy word for "handle." Made from wood or metal.

CROSS-PIECE
Stops an opponent's sword from cutting the hand you are fighting with.

BLADE
Two-sided, and stiffened by a ridge running down the centre.

POINT
A sharp, tapered blade designed for thrusting between your enemy's plates of armor.

PROS
- Great for thrusting
- You'll look like a real knight
- Use on foot or on a horse

CONS
- Expensive
- Not so good in a siege

LANCE

With the right skills, you can use a lance to skewer your enemy right through their armor, or at least knock them off their horse. In a jousting tournament, use a lance with a blunt end, called a coronal.

PROS
- Pierces through armor
- Looks intimidating

CONS
- Difficult to master
- Need a horse to use it
- Only useful for the first strike

TOP TIP
DON'T EVER BE TEMPTED TO USE AN OVERSIZED LANCE— IT MIGHT TOPPLE YOU OUT OF YOUR SADDLE.

PROS
- Stops arrows mid-flight
- Blocks sword blows

CONS
- Breaks easily
- One more thing to carry

SHIELD

Protect yourself from arrows and sword tips using a shield made from wood and leather. They bear your coat of arms, which is great in a tournament. But when you're fully clad in armor at war, you will have less need for one.

FALCHION

A falchion is like a sword, only more eye-catching. Its broad, curved blade might be short but still delivers a deadly blow.

PROS
- Smaller and lighter than a sword
- Eye-catching

CONS
- Awkward worn from a belt

MACE

A mace is a type of heavy club that is great for smashing things. If you can't find a mace, then a war hammer will do.

PROS
- Destroys helmets (and heads)
- Creates permanent damage

CONS
- Heavy to carry

BATTLE AXE

In the build-up to the Battle of Bannockburn, the Scottish king Robert the Bruce cleaved the head of Sir Henry de Bohun (an English knight) in two with one stroke of his axe. Grim!

PROS
- Lethal and deadly
- Has a point for piercing and a blade for slicing

CONS
- Very heavy to carry
- Makes a big mess

CROSSBOW

You will want to use a crossbow when you have a castle to defend. Choose the right size, depending on how far you need to fire. To load a crossbow, either hold it down with your foot and pull hard, or use a special winch.

PROS
- Good for defending castles
- Fires long distances

CONS
- Slow to load
- You need to be tall and strong to use it

SET TO WORK

Now you're suited and booted, you need someone to hire you. A good, steady job option is joining a retinue of knights who are all working for the same lord. Every knight is expected to bring their own horse, squires, servants and luggage.

STEP 1
CHOOSE A RETINUE

Joining a retinue isn't just for wartime. You'll also be expected to compete in tournaments and attend to your lord during peacetime. Look for a lord who is successful in the business of war, with a reputation for being generous with their wages.

LORD CHANCE-A-LOT NOW HIRING:

IF YOU WANT TO TAKE CHANCES WITH YOUR LIFE, JOIN MY RETINUE! I PAY GENEROUSLY IN CABBAGES AND OFFER 1 DAY A YEAR VACATION.

NEWLY TRAINED KNIGHTS FOR HIRE.
Have own horses, will travel.
CALL 020-KNIGHTS-IN-SHINING-ARMOR

STEP 2
SET YOUR WAGES

A knight's wages are not much of a reward considering how dangerous it is. If you're lucky, you may get paid two shillings per day in England, so consider working in Italy where there's more demand for soldiers. Although in England, you might receive a bonus called the regard, which is paid four times a year.

STEP 3
DRAW UP A JOB CONTRACT

Once you've chosen the lord you'd like to work for, make a written agreement, or contract, with them. The contract will either be for a single campaign, which you'll be paid for in cash, or for life, in which case you will receive a regular income or be paid in land.

HAPPY HORSE INSURANCE

For as little as 1 shilling a month*.
*Excluding vet fees.

STEP 4
INSURE YOUR HORSE

Your horse is a major investment. As soon as you get hired, get your horse valued in case it is killed in battle, or dies on campaign. Get as high a valuation as you can, so you have enough money to buy a new horse if something bad happens to your four-legged pal.

HOW TO GET A PROMOTION

THE BEST WAY TO MOVE UP THE RANKS IS TO BUILD YOUR OWN FOLLOWING.

ONCE YOU HAVE A RETINUE OF 20 OR MORE KNIGHTS WORKING FOR YOU, YOU'LL BECOME A BANNERET.

THE BLACK PRINCE HAD A RETINUE OF 11 BANNERETS, 102 KNIGHTS, 264 SQUIRES AND MEN-AT-ARMS AND 966 ARCHERS. THAT'S A LOT OF WAGES TO PAY!

Getting a promotion sounds expensive!

47

TOURNAMENT TIME

Battles are actually quite rare, so tournaments between two retinues of knights are a great way to practice your fighting. They're not nearly as dangerous, and your chivalrous acts will be seen by an entire audience instead of going unnoticed in the chaos of war. There are two compulsory days of dancing and drinking beforehand so expect plenty of noise.

TODAY:
OLD ENGLAND TOURNAMENT CLUB
MAY 5, 1343
LIONS VS FROGS
Featuring Geoffroi de Charny as the celebrity judge!

LET THE FIGHTING BEGIN...

The two sides are held back in separate areas, marked off by ropes. When the word is given, the ropes are cut, and off they go!

49

THE JOUSTING COMPETITION

If you want to become a knight who is famous for their courage and skill, enter a jousting competition. Jousts are fought between two individual knights who ride directly at one another on horseback.

SCORING
Ways of scoring vary from event to event. The top score is normally awarded for unhorsing your opponent; breaking a lance is the next best action; while striking your opponent on the helmet comes third.

JOUSTING DO'S AND DON'TS

Jousting is a highly skillful sport and requires a lot of concentration. Even the simplest slipup can be disastrous.

DON'TS

- Don't tilt your lance up or down—keep it aimed at your opponent
- Don't turn your shoulder to protect yourself—you'll only fall off
- Don't close your eyes on impact—watch your opponent's every move!

DO'S

- Control your horse—if it veers off course and takes you away from your opponent, you're doomed
- Use a light lance—too heavy and it will tip you off your horse
- Put your helmet on straight so that you can see

MAN OF THE MATCH

Prizes are awarded for breaking the most lances and keeping your helmet on the longest. But "man of the match" goes to the knight who delivers the best blow of all. Winners can walk away with a velvet cap or even a greyhound wearing a gold collar.

LET'S GO ON CAMPAIGN!

Now that you're trained and ready to show off your chivalric deeds, it's time to set out on a campaign to battle your enemy.

You and your fellow knights will ride the distance to your enemy's territory—spare a thought for your foot soldiers who will have to walk.

The trumpets are blasted once to signal it's time to saddle up.

The second trumpet blast means "eat now or forever hold your peace."

Banners are held at the front of the march to show everyone where to go.

The whole army will spread out over miles of countryside, rather than in a set order, and there will be lots of stragglers.

The third trumpet blast means "put on your armor and take up your weapons."

The fourth and final trumpet blast means "Let's go!"

THE TRUTH ABOUT
CAMPAIGNING

> You've set out on campaign now, so it's time to tell you the truth: much of your time as a knight will be spent riding through the countryside just trying to find your enemy.

> Onward, mighty knights!

> Thank goodness horses can swim!

THE WEATHER MATTERS

You won't have much choice, but it's best to go when the weather's good and food is plentiful, such as in the late summer. If you find yourself in the field any later in the year, then you might also have to battle with mud, snow and an empty stomach.

CAMP FOOD IS BARELY FOOD

On campaign an army has to live off the land—you might have plenty to eat today but nothing tomorrow. If you don't mind moldy bread and meat that crawls, then you'll love war food! But watch out for grit in your bread—it will grind your teeth down flat.

YOU MIGHT NOT GET A BED

As the army marches, a soldier will be sent ahead to find a place to rest for the night—hopefully in a town or village where the houses can be borrowed. A marshal should tell you where to sleep, but usually it's first come, first served. If you miss out, don't count on getting a tent either. Sleep under the stars and hold onto your horse's reins.

IT CAN BE QUITE BORING

There's a lot of work to be done when an army musters, or assembles, before battle. Lists have to be drawn up of the soldiers involved and their pay agreed before they are put into battalions. All of this can take several days, so you may have some time to fill.

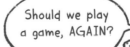

Should we play a game, AGAIN?

HOW TO PICK A FIGHT

I'm ROBERT THE BRUCE, King of Scotland, and I know a thing or two about picking fights. If you set out on campaign and your enemy refuses to fight you, here are some tips on how to force them into battle...

TIP #1
SET FIRE TO THEIR HOUSES

Once you've found your enemy, the way to really hurt them is to destroy their territory by setting it alight. Wooden houses are easy to set fire to, and even stone ones have flammable wooden floors and thatched roofs. Take inspiration from the Black Prince, who was a notorious arsonist. He burned down 11 cities and 3,700 villages on a raid in southern France.

TIP #2
RANSOM THE VILLAGERS

Killing villagers is a good way to frighten everyone. But there's no need to kill them all when you could ransom them instead. Even peasants can be made to pay for their freedom.

TIP #3
STEAL THEIR LIVESTOCK

Don't bother with individual animals—look for herds of cattle and sheep on the estate of a wealthy monastery. The monks will buy the stock back, at which point you can go and steal them again!

KNIGHT'S DISCLAIMER

PILLAGE AND PLUNDER ARE NECESSARY IN WAR. WHILE SUCH ACTIONS TECHNICALLY GO AGAINST THE CHIVALRIC CODE, THEY WILL NOT BE COUNTED AGAINST YOU IF PERFORMED AS AN ACT OF WAR. (ALTHOUGH AS KNIGHTS YOU SHOULD GET YOUR FOOT SOLDIERS TO DO ALL THE DIRTY WORK FOR YOU.)

PRE-BATTLE PEP TALK

You've annoyed your enemy enough now that they really want a fight. Before you set out, make sure your army is mentally prepared.

MAKE A SPEECH

You have to be in the right mood to fight, so give your soldiers a good pep talk before battle—and speak loudly! In the open air it's not so easy to hear over the noise of horses whinnying and men preparing their weapons. Failing this, just tell your army you're prepared to die for your country—they might just be inspired.

What did he just say?

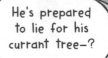

He's prepared to lie for his currant tree—?

58

RECITE A POEM

If you're good with words and have a talent for acting, why not recite a poem on the theme of loyalty and honor? Your soldiers might not understand every word, but if you deliver it with emotion, they will be moved to action!

For you my
NOBLE KNIGHTS,
there is no labor painful,
no place invincible,
no ground unpassable,
no hill however high inaccessible,
no tower unscalable,
no army impenetrable,
no soldier in arms or
host of men formidable.

SET OUT THE RULES

If you don't have a way with words, it might just be easier to set down some rules. Remind everyone that killing a soldier fighting on the same side—including yourself—is punishable by death. It won't boost morale but it will focus your soldiers' minds on the job at hand.

✗ **DO NOT** ride off without receiving an order
✗ **DO NOT** walk in front of the banners
✗ **DO NOT** shout out an order you are not entitled to give
✗ **DO NOT** ransom a prisoner without permission
✗ **DO NOT** strike or kill your companion-in-arms
✗ **DO NOT** kill yourself

59

PREPARE FOR BATTLE...

As a brave knight, you will want to fight in a battle.
But before you ride into the fight, it's best to plan your
tactics in advance. Why not draw up a plan that shows
where you'll position your foot soldiers and archers?
Plot where your reserves will be, and decide how
you'll defend all positions.

Put them back, Angus, they play a key role in our battle strategy.

BAGGAGE
AND HORSES

VALLE

ENGLISH
ARMY

TOP TIP

PICK YOUR BATTLEFIELD

Make sure that the ground is in good condition. Too boggy and it will be hard work for the horses. Vertical drops can be useful if you want to lead your enemy into a death-pit, while stone walls and hedges create quite effective defenses. If the terrain is tricky, dig small pits in the ground to trip up the enemy as they charge.

FRENCH ARMY

LEAD THE CHARGE!

As a knight, you will want to start a battle fighting on horseback, leading the charge. But it may be more sensible to follow the English example and fight on foot. That way, you can help your comrades and they can help you.

Steel your nerves everyone!

- When you charge, start slowly and stay in line with your fellow knights—never gallop ahead on your own.

- Only put your spurs on your horse when the enemy is in close range.

- Watch out for foot soldiers with pole weapons who might try to attack your horse.

- If you break through the enemy's line and out the other side, turn around and charge at them again from behind.

FIGHT FOR YOUR LIVES

Once the armies engage, you'll find yourself in a chaotic fighting mess. Now is the time to pull out your sword.

Your lance is likely to break on first impact. Throw it away—it's no more useful than a stick.

Stick together—getting separated from your army can be very dangerous.

Watch out for arrows—a trained archer can shoot 12 arrows every minute. If you hear a hissing sound, duck for cover!

If you're lucky, there will be a half-time break so everyone can catch their breath. Battles can last up to a few hours.

65

WHAT CAN GO WRONG?!

A lot, actually. But don't let that ruin your confidence—this is all just part of being a knight.

1. Your enemies might turn your own weapons on you.

GULP! If only I hadn't just sharpened my sword!

SHAME!

We do it my way—I've written a best-selling book on this, you know!

2. You might fall out with fellow soldiers and be unable to decide on tactics mid-battle.

AWKWARD...

3. You could fall off your horse and then have to fight on foot, possibly without weapons.

Thumb war, anyone?

OUCH!

4. If you march into battle, then you might be too exhausted and in no state to fight on foot.

TOO BAD

Just a minute. I need to catch my breath!

5. In the panic you may get trampled by your own colleagues, leading to suffocation.

TOTAL BUMMER...

6. You might get captured by the enemy, who will enjoy making fun of you in public.

EPIC FAIL!!!

DON'T BE A HERO

On the first day at the Battle of Bannockburn in Scotland, 1314, the "bold of heart and hand" knight William Deyncourt galloped all alone into the lines of Scottish foot soldiers. He was killed before anyone thought to ransom him.

ALWAYS REMEMBER: ONE MAN CANNOT DEFEAT AN ARMY.

So true.

67

RANSOMS AND BOOTY

War is big business! There's money to be made, but you need to weigh the risks. You can do very well from ransoms. You can also earn a bit of extra income by forcing villages and towns to pay you to protect them. If there's booty for the taking, you can make a fortune!

Can I get you a cup of tea?

HOW TO TAKE A PRISONER

You need to be careful not to injure your opponent too badly in the heat of battle, as a dead prisoner is worth nothing. Try and treat their wounds and don't let the common soldiers get to them!

KNOW THEIR VALUE

Don't listen to tall stories about prisoners who fetch high prices. If your prisoner is that important, it won't be up to you to determine the ransom anyway. You'll have to hand them over to the king, and he'll decide how much you get!

Geoffroi, I've caught a Queen!!

That's our Queen, Angus!! Pardon, Your Highness.

KNOW THE EXCHANGE RATES

Exchange rates rise and fall like yo-yos but as a general rule, a franc, a mouton d'or, an écu, a florin, a ducat and the Castilian dobla are all gold coins that are fairly similar in value.

SELL YOUR RANSOM QUICKLY

Get rid of any prisoners as fast as you can by selling them to a trader. You may not get the highest price, but at least you'll have made some money. Otherwise you risk getting stuck with the burden of paying for their food and care while you hold them prisoner.

RANSOMS AND BOOTY CONT'D

Not again...

HOW TO PAY YOUR OWN RANSOM

Even great soldiers get taken prisoner—just look at Geoffroi! You too might get captured and have a ransom to pay. If you're important enough, someone will help to pay this on your behalf. Royalty or bankers may come to your aid, your troops may start a fundraiser, or you may have a rich spouse to buy your freedom. Failing any of these, you could use land as payment or raise the funds yourself.

PROTECTION MONEY

If you're occupying part of a country, you can force the local peasants to pay you protection money. (Basically tell them you won't ransack their place if they pay you!) If the peasants don't cough up, then just imprison them and burn their property.

COLLECTING BOOTY

If you're successful in war, there's plenty of booty to be had! When the French town of Caen was sacked there wasn't a matron in England who wasn't dressed in fabrics from the raid. Your soldiers will become skilled treasure hunters, searching cellars, storehouses and barns.

WAS IT WORTH IT?

Although it might seem like you're rolling in money, you should be careful not to spend it immediately. Your lord will take at least a third of what you earn and you may have taxes to pay, leaving you with a tiny amount of winnings.

GO ON A CRUSADE!

Crusades are religious wars that Christians mostly started against Muslims, traveling from Europe to a variety of Islamic nations. With the blessing of the Pope, you are entitled to travel, plunder and pillage all on one vacation!

QUICK AND EASY GETAWAYS TO THE AFTERLIFE!

POPE CLEMENT V'S
TRAVEL GUIDE
FOR BUDDING
CRUSADERS

REWARDS IN HEAVEN GUARANTEED!

WISH YOU WERE HERE

THE **TOP PLACES** TO TROT,
BEFORE YOU LOSE YOUR SABATONS!

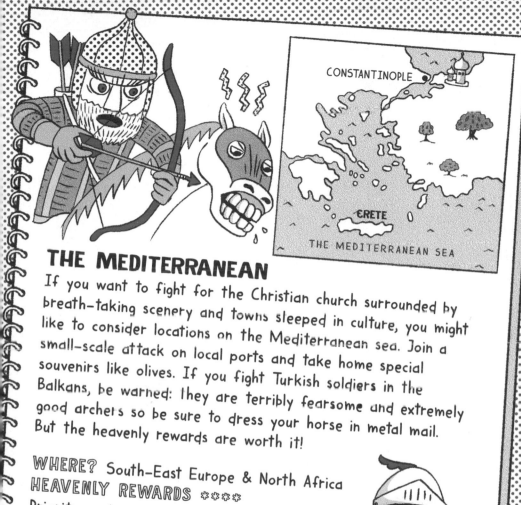

THE MEDITERRANEAN

If you want to fight for the Christian church surrounded by breath-taking scenery and towns sleeped in culture, you might like to consider locations on the Mediterranean sea. Join a small-scale attack on local ports and take home special souvenirs like olives. If you fight Turkish soldiers in the Balkans, be warned: they are terribly fearsome and extremely good archers so be sure to dress your horse in metal mail. But the heavenly rewards are worth it!

WHERE? South-East Europe & North Africa
HEAVENLY REWARDS ****
Priority seating in Heaven two rows back from Saint Peter, with a view of Christ our Lord and the Heavenly Father himself!!

TRAVEL TIP

If battle is aborted, strip off your armor, slap on some sunscreen and just chill. The weather here is gorgeous!

73

SPAIN

The Muslim Moors have been in retreat for many years as the kingdoms of Aragon, Castile and Portugal have steadily been expanded by Christians. Try to conquer the Emirate of Granada, which is still under Muslim rule. Beware though, as the Moors are dangerous opponents and well-trained to fight crusaders.

WHERE? Southwestern Europe
HEAVENLY REWARDS *****
Get fast-tracked at the Pearly Gates and be the first to board the stairway to Heaven!

TRAVEL TIP

You may be pleasantly surprised by how many Moorish habits the Christians have adopted. Spend your free time enjoying the public baths in any one of the Spanish cities.

THE BALTIC

Pope Clement V welcomes crusaders who are willing to continue the fight against pagans. Crusades in the Baltic are much safer than in the Mediterranean because most of the territory is taken, but the pagans still haven't been converted. There's not much booty to be had, and anything you do take is likely to be grabbed by the Teutonic Knights who have settled here almost permanently to enjoy the delicious food and fine furs.

WHERE? Northeastern Europe
HEAVENLY REWARDS ✱✱✱
Your star in Heaven will shine bright 24-7 and be visible even through cloud cover.

TRAVEL TIP
Bring an extra saddlebag for your shopping. There isn't much to plunder but you can purchase a nice fur coat for a reasonable price.

GET HIRED AS A MERCENARY

If you really want to be a knight but the pay is too stingy, you might want to consider becoming a mercenary. You don't need a noble or knightly background, and there are lots of jobs throughout Europe, fighting for other lords.

JOB INTERVIEW TIPS

★ LEARN ANOTHER LANGUAGE

You won't get far if you can't speak a few languages. If you want a warrior to surrender, then you need to tell them so—waving your arms around will only make them confused.

FRENCH
GERMAN
ITALIAN
LATIN

★ NEGOTIATE LIKE A PRO

Prepare to be tough when you're negotiating your pay and be careful to check you're not being ripped off. Charge extra for "dead lances"— soldiers killed on the job—and lost horses.

$

★ FORGET CHIVALRY

The most important thing as a mercenary is to show loyalty to your employer, not to the chivalric code. If they ask you to slaughter, plunder and pillage then you must.

WANTED

PART-TIME MERCENARY FOR
WERNER OF URSLINGEN

COMPANY: St. George

RESPONSIBLE FOR: Ravaging and pillaging

SKILLS REQUIRED: Brave, brutal and an excellent rider

LOCATION: Northern Italy

PAY: $$$$

When the German emperor Henry VII died on Italian soil, his knights remained in Italy and formed the Company of St. George. Now led by Werner of Urslingen, these German mercenaries are ravaging their way through northern Italy with plans to return home to Germany flush with cash. It's believed there are at least 3,500 German mercenaries in Italy so it's highly competitive. When you're being interviewed, think about how you stand out from the crowd.

At the interview...

I haven't killed anyone yet and I don't really want to, but I'm much better at riding now.

We'll call you...

WANTED

PART-TIME MERCENARY FOR
HUGH MORTIMER

COMPANY: The White Company
RESPONSIBLE FOR:
Devising battle tactics
SKILLS REQUIRED:
Shouting and arguing
LOCATION: Various, depending
on whose side we've taken
PAY: $$

If you love politics, you'll enjoy watching the English flit from one side to another, as their companies of mercenaries fall out with each other and get back together. When companies can't find employment, such as during the current time of truce between the English and the French, it can be problematic. Mercenaries start acting on their own, robbing and pillaging at every chance, whatever land they're in.

At the interview...

I got an At in debating and my voice carries across the whole playground, apparently.

You're HIRED!

WANTED

PART-TIME MERCENARY FOR
GUIDORICCIO DA FOGLIANO

COMPANY: Della Scala Family
RESPONSIBLE FOR: Recording musters and filing paperwork
SKILLS REQUIRED: Must be able to speak at least 2 languages
LOCATION: Italy
PAY: $$$

Foreign mercenaries do well in Italy. However, recently Italians are taking more of a leading role in the mercenary companies. (Don't worry if you're not Italian—there are still plenty of opportunities.) Guidoriccio da Fogliano is an important Italian mercenary, from a noble family in Reggio Emilia. He's quite friendly with Werner of Urslingen and sometimes joins forces with him. Fogliano is so important that there's even a painting of him on a palace wall in Siena!

At the interview...

I'm handsome, adaptable, and I speak both Italian and German. And some Latin!

Certo? Va bene!

Huh?

WOULD YOU RATHER BE A DAMSEL?

Damsels might not fight, but they do play a very important role in battle. A damsel's devotion will inspire and persuade a knight to do great things on campaign and on the battlefield. We can also seek the occasional pardon.

WHAT TO EXPECT FROM YOUR KNIGHT

As a damsel, you should expect to be loved, protected and honored. Settle for nothing less. A good knight will be prepared to die for you and won't just be after your wealth.

He loves me! He loves me not. He loves me!

Do you want the other sleeve, too?

WHAT'S EXPECTED OF YOU

Never encourage your knight to make dangerous or unrealistic vows. Instead, send your knight practical presents as well as symbols of your devotion. Include a few warhorses with your love letters, or detach the sleeve of your gown and tie it to your knight's helmet or lance—in return they'll be expected to perform noble deeds in your name.

We're here for you John!

CHEER ON YOUR CHAMPION

The great part of being a damsel is that you'll be involved in a tournament! You'll lead the knights in processions, cheer them on, and get to enjoy the dinners and dances. You may even win a prize for your dance moves, such as a golden brooch or diamond ring!

I ♥ JOHN

LADIES TAKE CHARGE

LADIES WHO LEAD

If being a damsel isn't your thing, take inspiration from the wife of the English knight Robert Knollys. She took an active part in the war— even leading the troops—and joined her husband's expeditions, taking their children with her. There's also a group of young women in England who dress up as men and compete in tournaments. Although highly illegal, it's a great option if you're feeling left out of the action.

81

MEDIEVAL MEDICARE

The challenge that all knights face is to boldly go on adventures and fight battles despite how risky and uncomfortable they may be. And when things go really wrong, not to give up hope.

DON'T GO TO THE DOCTOR

Avoid seeking medical care on campaign whenever possible. If you do need it, ask for a stick to bite on. If you really need a surgeon, find one with military experience who has written a textbook or two. It's useful to have someone who knows what they're doing if you have a limb that needs amputating, or a crossbow bolt in your knee...

GET TO THE BOTTOM OF IT

If you spend too long in the saddle, then you might end up with a rather unpleasant condition, too uncomfortable to talk about. The main treatment, apart from surgery, is the use of enemas. If you don't like sticking things up your bottom, then a hot bath might just have to do!

GET COVERED IN POOP

As odd as this may sound, it might be your only option if you fall into a freezing cold river or castle moat and need to be revived. The warmth of the poop is the medieval equivalent of a safety blanket.

THE PLAGUE

If battle doesn't kill you, then the plague might. Outbreaks can kill half a population, or more. However, there is nothing you can do about it. No one in the 14th century understands the cause, and doctors have no cure.

Humans! They have no idea how good fleas are at carrying disease!

HEAVEN OR HELL?

When you die, you will either end up in heaven or hell. In hell you will be nailed into your armor and have to wear it from dusk to dawn, and be forced to take baths with slimy toads. Follow this advice to avoid the fiery pits:

PAY YOUR WAY TO HEAVEN

You may have to burn down a few churches in your career so to save your soul, donate generously to your local church and then they'll pray for you once you're dead. 50,000 masses should be enough to guarantee a happy afterlife.

CHOOSE A TOMB

A good tomb will mean you're remembered for years to come. A cheap option is a memorial brass, which is a standard engraving of a knight wearing the latest style of armor. A life-size effigy, or model, is a grander choice, especially if it is lifelike. Make sure the artist is experienced and has good eyesight.

Can you make my legs a bit longer?

Is this his other foot?

It'll do.

MAKE RESURRECTION PLANS

If you hope to be resurrected and come back to life, try to be buried in one piece. If parts of your body have to be collected from various places, there's a risk that you may end up with something missing, or not belonging to you.

WRITE YOUR MEMOIRS

Your knightly deeds will be remembered for all time if a book is written about you. If you're lucky enough to meet French author Jean Froissart, he might write about you in his chronicles. Alternatively, you could take a leaf out of Pedro IV of Aragon's book and write an autobiography.

I'll call it "My glorious career as a knight in not-very-shiny-armor."

IF WARRIOR LIFE APPEALS,
BUT YOU'RE NOT CONVINCED YOU'RE
THE CHIVALROUS TYPE,
TURN TO PAGE 96 FOR OTHER
ANCIENT JOB OPTIONS!

SCOTLAND

IRELAND

ENGLAND

NORTH
SEA

LONDON

FRANCE

HOLY
ROMAN
EMPIRE

ATLANTIC
OCEAN

Seine

Rhine

N

PORTUGAL

CASTILE

ARAGON

MEDITERRANEAN
SEA

ROME

GRANADA

SARDINIA

TUNIS

88

MAP OF MEDIEVAL EUROPE

Where would you like to go on campaign?

LITHUANIA

GDAŃSK

POLAND

Danube

HUNGARY

BLACK SEA

CONSTANTINOPLE

MEDITERRANEAN SEA

SICILY

RHODES

CYPRUS

GLOSSARY

AKETON a padded jacket, worn by itself, or combined with mail or plate armor

AVENTAIL a curtain of mail attached to a helmet that covers the throat, neck and shoulders

BACINET a pointed helmet, often with a visor

BANNERET the military rank, above a knight

BATTALION a large group of troops, ready for battle

BATTERING RAM a long, heavy pole used to break down castle gates

BOOTY goods captured in war

CAMPAIGN one or more planned battles—to invade or loot another country

CHAMFRON protective armor for a horse's head

CHIVALRY the preferred behavior of knights based on honor, kindness and courage

CIVILIAN a person not in the armed forces

CLERK a person employed to keep good records and do other admin

COAT OF ARMS symbol or design, often on a shield, that represents a particular family

CORONAL the blunt end of a tournament lance

CRUSADE a series of military expeditions led by the Christian church

CUIRASS armor where the breastplate and backplate fasten together

DAMSEL a young lady

EXPEDITION a journey undertaken by a group of people with a specific purpose, such as war

FALCHION a broad, slightly curved sword

GARRISON a group of troops defending a castle or town

GARTER a piece of clothing for the leg, strangely used by Edward III as the symbol of his order of knighthood

GAUNTLET an armored glove

HEDGING when a masterless knight "wanders" and sleeps under hedges

HOLY LAND the land of Israel in the eastern Mediterranean

JOUST to duel with a lance while on horseback

KING ARTHUR a legendary British leader during the late 5th and early 6th centuries

KNIGHTED the act of giving someone the rank of knight

KNIGHTHOOD the rank of a knight

LANCE a long weapon made of a wooden pole and a steel point, used by horsemen when charging

LATIN language of ancient Rome, used for education and admin

MAIL armor of linked metal rings

MARSHAL a high-ranking officer in the household of a prince or lord

MERCENARY a soldier who fights for any country that pays them

MONKS religious men who promise to stay poor, to worship God every day, and never get married

MOORS Muslim people of northwestern Africa, who later settled in Spain

MUSTER the gathering of troops at the start of a campaign

PAGAN a person who worships more than one god

PEASANT a poor farmer

PLATE ARMOR armor made up of metal sheets

PLUNDER stolen goods and money, or the act of taking those things— usually using violence

RANSOM payment to release a prisoner

RESURRECTION to return to life after death

RETINUE a group of people, such as servants and companions, who follow an important person

ROBERT THE BRUCE King of Scotland, 1306–1329

SABATONS armor for the feet

SIEGE when an army surrounds a town or city, cutting off food and water supplies—so those inside surrender

SIEGE ENGINE a large weapon of war, designed to break down or get around heavy doors or walls

SQUIRE a young nobleman who assists a knight before becoming one himself

TURKS Turkish-speaking people of the Ottoman Empire

VIGIL keeping awake, during a time of sleep

WAR HAMMER a hammer-shaped weapon: blunt on one side and spiked on the other

COATS OF ARMS

How do you tell friend from foe when you're on the battlefield? By becoming an expert at decoding coats of arms! Here's a handy guide to some of the coats of arms used in Medieval Europe.

ENGLAND
THREE LEOPARDS = BRAVE

IRELAND
GOLDEN HARP = NOBLE

SCOTLAND
RED LION = COURAGEOUS

FRANCE
FLEURS-DE-LIS (LILY FLOWER) = PURE

PORTUGAL
FIVE SHIELDS = STRONG IN BATTLE

POLAND
WHITE EAGLE = POWERFUL

LITHUANIA
KNIGHT ON HORSEBACK = BOLD HERO

SWEDEN
THREE CROWNS = ROYAL

Turn to page 30 to see how they are designed.

My mom's family are from Ireland. What does the harp mean?

It's a sign you are noble.

INDEX